# What Has

## By Pamela Chanko

ISBN: 978-1-338-88862-1

Editor: Liza Charlesworth
Art Director: Tannaz Fassihi; Designer: Tanya Chernyak
All photos © Shutterstock.com.

1 2 3 4 5 6 7 8 9 10   68   31 30 29 28 27 26 25 24 23
Printed in Jiaxing, China. First printing, January 2023.

# SCHOLASTIC INC.

What has wheels?
This green car has wheels.

What has wheels?
This yellow bus has wheels.

What has wheels?
This orange bike has wheels.

What has wheels?
This red truck has wheels.

What has wheels?
This blue van has wheels.

What has wheels?
This silver cart has wheels.

Who has wheels?
These cool kids have wheels!
ZOOM, ZOOM!